NEW KIDS ON THE BLOCK
NEW KIDS ON THE BLOCK
NEW KIDS ON THE BLOCK
NEW KIDS ON THE BLOCK
NEW KIDS ON THE BLOCK

A MESSAGE FROM THE NEW KIDS

A BIG HELLO to all you guys out there and welcome to the fun- and fact-filled pages of the NEW KIDS ON THE BLOCK annual. We really hope you like it. It's been a whirlwind kind of year for all of us, gigging the length and breadth of the States, flying to the UK and Europe, more gigs, TV interviews and meeting oh so many of our friends. Phew! – takes your breath away just sayin' it, but we had ourselves a ball. Yep, we sure did. We owe so much to all the folk that look after us in one way or another, from Maurice, our record producer, Dick Scott, our manager and all the guys at Dick Scott Entertainment who are our management company, way down to the backstage crew and everybody in between – they are all so, so important to us. But even more, we owe everything to you guys, our friends. We use the word 'friends' because that's what you are to us, not merely fans. We would like to take this chance to thank each and every one of you for supporting us and just being there when it really mattered. THANKS. We've got some mega-exciting plans afoot to make next year even better and, rest assured, we want you all to be part of it, 'CAUSE WE LOVE YA!!!!! – yes, we do. Hope you have as much fun reading this book as we did putting it together for you.

So, you all take care and

HANG TOUGH COVERGIRL,
'CAUSE WE'LL BE LOVIN' YOU FOREVER.

Written by Tommy Jay with
additional material by Kim Glover.

Designed by Hilary Edwards,
Liz Auger and Bob Swan.

Published in Great Britain by
World International Publishing Limited,
An Egmont Company, Egmont House,
P.O. Box 111, Great Ducie Street,
Manchester M60 3BL.
Printed in Italy ISBN 0 7235 6904 5

CONTENTS

THE STORY SO FAR.....

Whilst they are mega-famous in America and set to conquer the rest of the world in the very near future, the NEW KIDS haven't always had it easy, all of them living in and around the tough neighbourhoods of Boston, Massachusetts. Growing up on the streets they soon learned how to look after themselves. Says Donnie, "It was the only way to survive out there." They've all had friends with criminal records for various offences and reckon that without the intervention of a certain Mr Starr they could easily have walked down the wrong side of the street. However, fate had other ideas.

Danny hangin' out with Maurice

At about the time this was all going down and the guys were getting into all sorts of scrapes, Maurice Starr was having a few problems himself. Maurice is a record producer, songwriter and music biz entrepreneur and he was in legal wrangles with his band NEW EDITION. Bobby Brown was leaving to concentrate on a solo career and things in general weren't going well, so he decided that it was time to put together a new outfit with which to assault the charts. Five talented kids who could sing, dance, write and play music as well as look real cool were the order of the day, so Maurice set to work.

Donnie was the first on the scene and he introduced Danny Wood, an old school pal. Danny pulled in Jordan Knight and Jordan suggested his brother Jonathan. Jamie Kelly was the other original member, but he didn't quite fit in and was replaced by Joseph McIntyre. This was back in 1984 and whilst Maurice wrote some killer songs the guys were working on dance routines and polishing up their stage act.

After a lot of hard work and heartache the guys were eventually ready to roll. Called NYNUK at this point, they started doing gigs around Boston. Some went well, others not so good, but they had all developed a burning desire to succeed and it was beginning to show that maybe Maurice had got the chemistry right and the guys really were going to be something special.

The name NYNUK was hated by everybody so it was decided to change the name to the title of one of the songs they did on stage, and the NEW KIDS ON THE BLOCK were born.

The giant CBS record company signed the band and launched them on an unsuspecting public at the Statue of Liberty Festivities on 4th July in New York. The NEW KIDS' first album was initially no great success, but it has consequently sold over two and a half million copies. It wasn't until February 1989 that NKOTB had the first heady aroma of success in their nostrils, when YOU GOT IT (THE RIGHT STUFF) climbed strongly into the American Hot 100, followed in June of the same year by their first US No 1, I'LL BE LOVIN' YOU FOREVER. HANGIN' TOUGH was next to reach the coveted top slot and the second album was selling like it was going out of fashion. Not bad for five young guys from the streets of Boston, eh?

Hangin' Tough: the first album from NKOTB

.....THE STORY

Touring is a very major part of the NEW KIDS' lives, and they got the chance to play bigger and better venues when pop songstress TIFFANY asked them to join her on her tour of America. The guys all have a great respect for TIFFANY and to this day remain the best of pals with her. TIFFANY has since signed with the NEW KIDS management.

The Christmas album and the single THIS ONE'S FOR THE CHILDREN saw in the new decade with the NEW KIDS ON THE BLOCK firmly entrenched in the American top ten. But now they were setting their sights on the rest of the world – starting with the UK. Two No 1's, two top ten singles and a mega-successful album were the kick-off point for a tour and the NEW KIDS were received in a BEATLES-like fashion. (The BEATLES were the first mega-successful band back in the '60s. They got mobbed everywhere they went too!) With the help of their ultra-shrewd manager, DICK SCOTT, they went from the UK into Europe. More gigs, television appearances and interviews with radio and press followed and it seemed like NEW KIDS ON THE BLOCK were unstoppable. That's what we all think anyway, isn't it, gang?

SO FAR.....

The guys worked hard and were so busy that their new album had to be recorded whilst they were on the road. Again, Maurice Starr wrote, arranged and put down the backing tracks. Then the NEW KIDS went into studios local to the gigs to add their voices and their production ideas when they got off stage, often working right into the early hours of the morning.

This last tour has been buzzin' around the US, the UK and Europe for over two years now and the NEW KIDS don't get home that much, but even so, they still love doing the gigs and meeting all their fans. Being, without doubt, the hottest pop property in the world it's nice to be able to report that they are still the same people they were before superstardom overtook them. Donnie says that the friends they had before they were famous are really important since they aren't just there because of the money. The guys being fairly mega-rich now, it would be easy to pick up a lot of hangers-on. The future is looking pretty bright too, and loads more gigs and many more hits are sure to figure highly.

12

FACT FILE ON DANNY

FULL NAME	Daniel William Wood Jr
DATE AND PLACE OF BIRTH	14th May 1970 in Boston, Massachusetts
COLOUR OF HAIR	Black
COLOUR OF EYES	Dark brown
HEIGHT	5'7"
WEIGHT	10st 5lbs
STAR SIGN	Taurus
FAMILY	Mother: a nurse Father: a mailman Four sisters: Beth, Melissa, Pam and Rachel One brother: Brett
LIVES NOW	Boston, Massachusetts
MARITAL STATUS	Single
HOBBIES	Danny enjoys workin' out in the gym
FAVOURITE CAR	Jeep
FAVOURITE CLOTHES	Nike tracksuits
FAVOURITE MUSIC	Maurice Starr, NEW KIDS ON THE BLOCK
LUCKY CHARM	Stuffed tiger called Tigger
IDEAL LADY	Must have a sense of humour, and be understanding. This lifestyle is tough on a relationship...

Last year they earned as much as one of their all-time heroes, Michael Jackson, and made more from merchandising (T-shirts, programmes, badges etc) than the Rolling Stones did on their last tour.

Danny, Donnie and Jordan work together as a songwriting team.

Jordan has a lucky bracelet which he has worn non-stop for six years.

In their home state of Massachusetts, 22nd April has been declared NEW KIDS' day.

Donnie considers it bad luck to shave before a show.

Jonathan likes to wear K-Swiss trainers.

The Hi-Fi Pizza restaurant was where the guys started their careers.

Donnie once worked in the foreign exchange department in a bank and won an award for never being late.

Jonathan keeps exotic fish.

ordan really loves to hear the fans screaming and shouting when he is on stage. He says hat it pushes him to give that much more in his performance.

All of the NEW KIDS will have nothing to do with drugs of any kind. It's a negative thing, they say, and have seen the effects it can have at close quarters.

Donnie sometimes talks too much in interviews and the others have to shut him up.

The NEW KIDS are set to become movie stars in the very near future.

Danny is never happier than when he's playin' basketball.

The NEW KIDS' families are also involved with the band. Their mums run the American fan club.

Their image is squeaky clean, but the guys won't admit to being angels. They reckon to be just ordinary folk, but with a very positive attitude to everything they do.

Jordan was a baseball pitcher and used to play in local league games.

Jordan and Danny wrote I'LL BE YOUR EVERYTHING with Tommy Page. It sold 500,000 copies and was a big hit.

Joseph is an avid collector of baseball caps.

Joseph has a shower before every show, no matter what.

16

FACT FILE ON JORDAN

FULL NAME	Jordan Nathaniel Marcel Knight
DATE AND PLACE OF BIRTH	17th May 1971 in Worcester, Massachusetts
COLOUR OF HAIR	Brown
COLOUR OF EYES	Brown
HEIGHT	5'10"
WEIGHT	11st
STAR SIGN	Taurus
FAMILY	Mother: a social worker Father: an Episcopal priest Two sisters: Allison and Sharon Three brothers: David, Chris and Jonathan
LIVES NOW	Boston, Massachusetts
MARITAL STATUS	Single
HOBBIES	Loves watching movies
FAVOURITE CAR	Porsche
FAVOURITE MUSIC	PRINCE, TEDDY RILEY
LUCKY CHARM	Six-year-old string bracelet
IDEAL LADY	Real cute and charming, but able to look after herself 'cause we tour a lot

KIDS' MANIA

MOBBED: The New Kids are besieged by fans at Heathrow airport. Pictur

IT'S GREAT TO SEE YOU, KIDS

LATEST POP sensations New Kids On The Block flew into London early yesterday morning to an hysterical welcome from 200 screaming girl fans at Heathrow Airport.

The scenes recalled the crazy days of Beatlemania as the American group arrived to begin their first UK tour.

Girls carrying "We Love You" banners and singing their songs went wild with deafening screams.

The group were swallowed up by the fans who raced forward as police and minders tried in vain to keep them away.

Some excited fans tried to grab at their idols as they were hustled through the airport.

But the New Kids weren't fazed by their chaotic welcome to the UK.

TIRED: Joe yesterday

By MIRROR REPORTER

As more girl fans – most of them playing truant from school – besieged their hotel after breakfast, lead singer Jon Knight, 21, vowed:

"We are going to give our British fans the best shows they have ever seen!

"We love Britain and our fans here are so special to us.

"We were up all last night talking to girls outside our window – even though we were jet-lagged!"

But the multi-millionaire band – in the charts with I'll be Loving You Forever – also have a serious message for fans along with the music.

They will use their tour to spread anti-drug warnings.

Jordan Knight, 19, said: "We have seen kids in our neighbourhood messed up by drugs, and we don't want that to happen to our fans.

"We tell them not to touch drugs."

But he added: "We're not squeaky clean. We're real –just ask the girls!"

Teddy lays up New Kid

A FURRY toy knocked Danny Wood out of last night's New Kids On The Block concert.

He was sent sprawling the night before when a fan threw it on stage and he tripped, spraining an ankle.

A doctor yesterday ordered him to pull out of the Fab Five's show last night at Whitley Bay, Newcastle.

A spokesman said: "Pain killers are making him sleepy and he's been told to keep his leg up."

Danny, 20, will remain seated if he appears tonight.

Kids get the fans fainting

POP'S latest sensation, New Kids On The Block, had fans fainting last night as they blasted into Britain.

Ten teenies passed out and an impromptu display of the boys' torsos drew a deafening roar from the packed concert hall.

Tiny Joe McIntyre – t 16 the youngest member of the American nd – had to be rescued security guards when was pulled into the crowd at the Edinburgh Playhouse. Donny Osmond lookalike Jordon Knight took centre stage, singing throughout most of the show.

But each Kid sang a lead vocal on different songs – giving all fans a chance to scream at their favourites.

Thirteen-year-old Julie Summers said: "I used to like Bros but the New Kids are much better – and there's more of them."

"Quick! New blocks on the kid!"

Caught Live!

Girls go wild in New Kids mayhem

By PIERS MORGAN

THOUSANDS of screaming girls stormed pop idols New Kids on the Block at their first British show last night. The frenzied fans BOMBARDED their idols with knickers.

In the most amazing scenes since Beatlemania the American supergroup proved they are the hottest band around.

Dozens of security staff battled to keep control as more

KIDS SPOT

IF you don't have a ticket now, you will never get one. With one million applications for 100,000 tickets, Harvey Goldsmith said: "You can't even steal one!"

SIZZLING SUCCESS: New Kids Jon, Jordan, Joe, Donnie and Danny – mobbed by 8,000

Hot group's fans cool off with cubes

By GILL PRINGLE and SONIA LEGG

FANS of pop's hottest group swooned as temperatures soared yesterday.

So the frenzied youngsters, waiting to see American stars New Kids on the Block, were given **ICE CUBES** to cool them down.

Ambulancemen handed out the ice as scores of fans, known as Blockheads, fainted before the band even went on stage in Brighton.

Elsewhere in balmy Britain, sunbathers settled for cold drinks and ice-cream amid forecasts that there's still warmer weather to come this week.

A crowd of more than 8,000 had gathered for an early glimpse of the Kids, who were getting set for a Brighton concert last night.

Some girls had staged an all-day vigil outside the band's hotel.

But as temperatures rose into the 70s, fans began to wilt.

Screamed

A few screamed their idols' names – Joe McIntyre, Jon and Jordan Knight, Donnie Wahlberg and Danny Wood.

They were rewarded by the occasional appearance of a Kid on a hotel balcony.

Fan Mary Ingham, from Haywards Heath, said: "I fainted when I

Donnie . . . a frenzy

'Block' fever rises

TEENAGE fan fever surrounded pop sensation New Kids On the Block at the start of their British tour in Edinburgh last night.

Hundreds of frenzied fans, nicknamed "blockheads", waited for hours outside the chart-toppers' hotel as they prepared for their Playhouse show.

Police, security guards and some of the band's entourage had to stop fans entering the Caledonian hotel where the young American heart-throbs were staying.

And outside the show venue, crowds began gathering more than three hours before the sell-out concert began.

DDY bear turned teenybop hero Wood into a New Kid On The he left London in a wheelchair

izarre accident while on stage hester, the New Kids On The pped on a cuddly teddy thrown ell, tearing ankle ligaments.

y, 19, wanted to carry on with British tour, but doctors to the States to rest. "I can't happened. It's such a dumb aid, waving a cheery crutch ncorde at Heathrow.

y Riddell – Page 18

Here's the new kid on the crock!

th Co pip hor deo mo

Lo spok desc

da dec me par is sho

T Aut of "W the scre ing

Pr be a

C di du

w st h

NDARD

ds under siege as the girls go crazy

by Lesley O'Toole

MING girls who latest American pop on New Kids On The as they flew into nrow were today ed outside the group's t hotel.

"Fab Five" arrived late night for a sell-out UK their first in this country.

re than a dozen fans ped out overnight in the er cold. By breakfast time r numbers had swollen to re than fifty. One fan who had waited all night, Sarah Terry, aged 15, from Hackney, said that she had gone to the airport to see them arrive and was supposed to have been home by 11pm.

She said: "My mum doesn't know where I am. I haven't telephoned her or anything. I know she must be worried and she'll probably kill me when I get home, but I've done this for the New Kids to show them I love them."

The Kids, who are already said to have earned millions of dollars each, laughed off suggestions that they are only in it for the money.

"We're very lucky," said Donnie. "We are paid for doing what we love."

Asked what they found strangest about Britain, the five were unanimous: "Warm beer, fish-and-chips, no ice cubes, and those strange accents." Co-manager Dick Scott gave his verdict on the phenomenon.

"It's all down to charisma; they've got as much as the Beatles ever had."

While many may ponder the lifespan of America's latest pop export, Mr Scott seems philosophical: "Life is what it is; a few days of heaven, and then no more."

Pictures: CLIVE HOWES

Excited fans glimpse their heroes today

Britain goes balmy – and you ain't seen nothing yet

IT'S NEW KIDS ON THE ICE BLOCK

New Kids On The Block,

20 FACT FILE ON JONATHAN

FULL NAME	Jonathan Rashleigh Knight
DATE AND PLACE OF BIRTH	29th November 1969 in Worcester, Massachusetts
COLOUR OF HAIR	Brown
COLOUR OF EYES	Hazel
HEIGHT	5'11"
WEIGHT	11st
STAR SIGN	Sagittarius
FAMILY	Mother: a social worker Father: an Episcopal priest Two sisters: Allison and Sharon Three brothers: David, Chris and Jordan
LIVES NOW	Boston, Massachusetts
MARITAL STATUS	Single
HOBBIES	Looking after his shar pei puppy which has earned the nickname Wrinkles 'cause that's what it looks like
FAVOURITE CAR	BMW 735 (black)
FAVOURITE CLOTHES	His collection of 50 leather jackets - all of which he takes on the tour bus with him!
FAVOURITE MUSIC	GEORGE MICHAEL, BOBBY BROWN - in fact almost anything except heavy metal
IDEAL LADY	Successful in her own right, independent and a good looker

U.S.
GOLDEN
GLOVES

SQUARE

Search for the NEW KIDS in this wordsquare.

E	H	K	L	O	Y	W	M	S	L	X	D
D	O	L	N	E	W	K	I	D	S	O	J
N	C	B	K	J	O	N	A	T	H	A	N
B	K	H	I	O	N	N	D	E	N	D	N
I	N	T	N	R	E	J	O	S	E	P	H
V	E	N	E	D	A	N	N	Y	H	K	O
A	W	O	W	A	N	O	N	H	E	W	K
T	K	S	K	N	I	D	I	T	B	E	E
F	I	D	I	D	S	O	E	N	L	N	U
A	D	I	K	W	E	N	K	C	O	K	R
W	S	O	N	T	H	E	B	L	O	C	K
K	I	D	S	O	N	T	H	E	D	O	N

Answers on page 60

So you think you know about the NEW KIDS, huh? Well see how you make out with these questions. No peekin' at the answers!

1. What is the name of the band that Donnie manages?
2. Which one of the KIDS collects baseball caps?
3. How many No 1's did the KIDS have in the UK prior to June1990?
4. Who was the original fifth member of the band?
5. Maurice Starr is the band's producer/songwriter, but what was the name of his other band which featured Bobby Brown?
6. Jordan has a passion for a certain meal. What is it?
7. This KID is a 'take charge' kind of guy. Who is he?
8. A bit of a brain box. Who is he?
9. Who is the only KID with blue eyes?
10. Who has a very large collection of leather jackets?
11. Who was the very first NEW KID?
12. Watching movies is whose favourite pastime?
13. Flippin' pizzas was whose game?
14. What is special about 22nd April in Boston, Massachusetts?

Answers on page 60

FACT FILE ON DONNIE

FULL NAME	Donald E Wahlberg (the E don't mean nothin')
DATE AND PLACE OF BIRTH	17th August 1969 in Dorchester, Massachusetts
COLOUR OF HAIR	Blond
COLOUR OF EYES	Hazel
HEIGHT	5'11"
WEIGHT	11st
STAR SIGN	Leo
FAMILY	Mother: a nurse Father: a union man Three sisters: Debbie, Michelle and Tracy Four brothers: Mark, Paul Arthur, Robert and James
LIVES NOW	Boston, Massachusetts
MARITAL STATUS	Single
HOBBIES	Computer games, riding motorbikes
FAVOURITE CAR	Saab 90
FAVOURITE CLOTHES	NORTH SIDE POSSE jacket
FAVOURITE MUSIC	BOBBY BROWN, KARYN WHITE
IDEAL LADY	Someone who wants me, not my fame and fortune, with good looks and independence

IN THEIR

JORDAN Our fans are real important to us so we try to stay in touch with them if we can. Hey, they are the ones who made us what we are today, and we're real grateful.

JONATHAN I couldn't eat for a week before our first show. I was so nervous that when I went on stage my knees were knockin'.

DANNY Music has given us something to aim for. Being in the group is like belonging to a basketball team – it keeps you off the streets.

JOSEPH I think that I've missed out a bit, not going to a regular school. I used to be a pretty good student before we started touring, then all of a sudden it changed.

JORDAN If one of the other guys in the group likes the same girl I do, usually I'm the one that backs off and lets him go out with her.

DONNIE When I was a kid I was pretty wild.

DANNY Girls who I like make me nervous. I can't seem to talk to them.

JOSEPH Reading about myself in magazines makes me laugh a lot. I love it.

JONATHAN If we ain't careful, without the ozone layer we're all gonna fry.

DANNY I'm really into fitness and health. The others call me the food cop.

DONNIE I look at Joseph and see a younger version of me.

OWN WORDS

DONNIE Maybe our first record not doing too well was good for us – we tasted failure and perhaps learned how to avoid it.

JONATHAN We all come from large families. Donnie and Joseph have nine in theirs and me, Danny and Jordan have six in ours.

JOSEPH It's real tough being on the road all the time but it's such a positive experience meeting all our fans.

DANNY The most important quality in any girl that I might want to go out with is that she must understand my schedule. It ain't easy havin' a boyfriend who is never there.

JORDAN My musical tastes were definitely influenced by my brothers and sisters 'cause when I was younger I didn't have any money to buy my own records so I wouid listen to theirs. That's why I think that Van Halen, Elton John and The Sugar Hill Gang are all great.

JONATHAN When we go home our mothers often read us letters from fans, because they handle our fan club in America.

DONNIE YO! England is real cool!!!

JOSEPH I get nervous before a concert, sometimes I get *real* nervous.

AND REMEMBER:
"IT AIN'T OVER TILL THE FAT LADY SINGS!"

”

FACT FILE ON JOSEPH

FULL NAME	Joseph Mulrey McIntyre
DATE AND PLACE OF BIRTH	31st December 1972 in Needham, Massachusetts
COLOUR OF HAIR	Light brown
COLOUR OF EYES	Blue
HEIGHT	5'6"
WEIGHT	8st 8lbs
STAR SIGN	Capricorn
FAMILY	Mother: a secretary Father: Vice-President of the Bricklayers' Union Seven sisters: Judy, Alice, Susan, Tricia, Carol, Jean and Kate One brother: Tommy
LIVES NOW	Boston, Massachusetts
MARITAL STATUS	Single
HOBBIES	Listening to OL' BLUE EYES (Frank Sinatra)
FAVOURITE CLOTHES	Charlet Hornets' baseball jacket
LUCKY CHARM	Silver chain with medallions
IDEAL LADY	An independent beauty who wants to live a good life and be happy

STEP BY STEP
MAKING THE VIDEO

The making of a video is a pretty complicated sequence of events. The original ideas are put on to paper in the form of a storyboard. This shows very basically what is going to happen and which part each of us will play. Many discussions take place and changes are often made to the storyboard until we are totally happy that the video will be just how we want it. That sounds fairly simple, but remember, this is all goin' down whilst we are still on tour, so as you can imagine telephone lines are really buzzin'. The next step is for the director and producer to start turning the ideas into reality. The location has to be found, the wardrobe organised and camera and lighting crews hired.

The day of the actual filming dawns and is bright and sunny — not that surprising since we are on location in California. As we arrive we're greeted by what looks like chaos. Hoards of technicians are running all over setting up the stacks of equipment and cameras. We say a quick 'hello' to the director then go to our dressing rooms where Brad, our make-up man, and Uncle Rob, who's in charge of our wardrobe, are waiting to get us ready. With clothes fitted and make-up done we start to warm up. We have worked out our dance routine with the choreographer, but practice makes perfect, so we run through it several times while we're waiting to be called to the set. Each of us has his own little part to play in the video. Joseph will be dressed in a tail suit, Danny will be workin' out (isn't he always?), Donnie will ride about on a motorcycle, Jordan will dance and Jonathan will play the part of a director. Rehearsals take up the rest of the morning. We run through everything in detail to perfect our performance, while the director puts the cameramen and the rest of the crew through their paces.

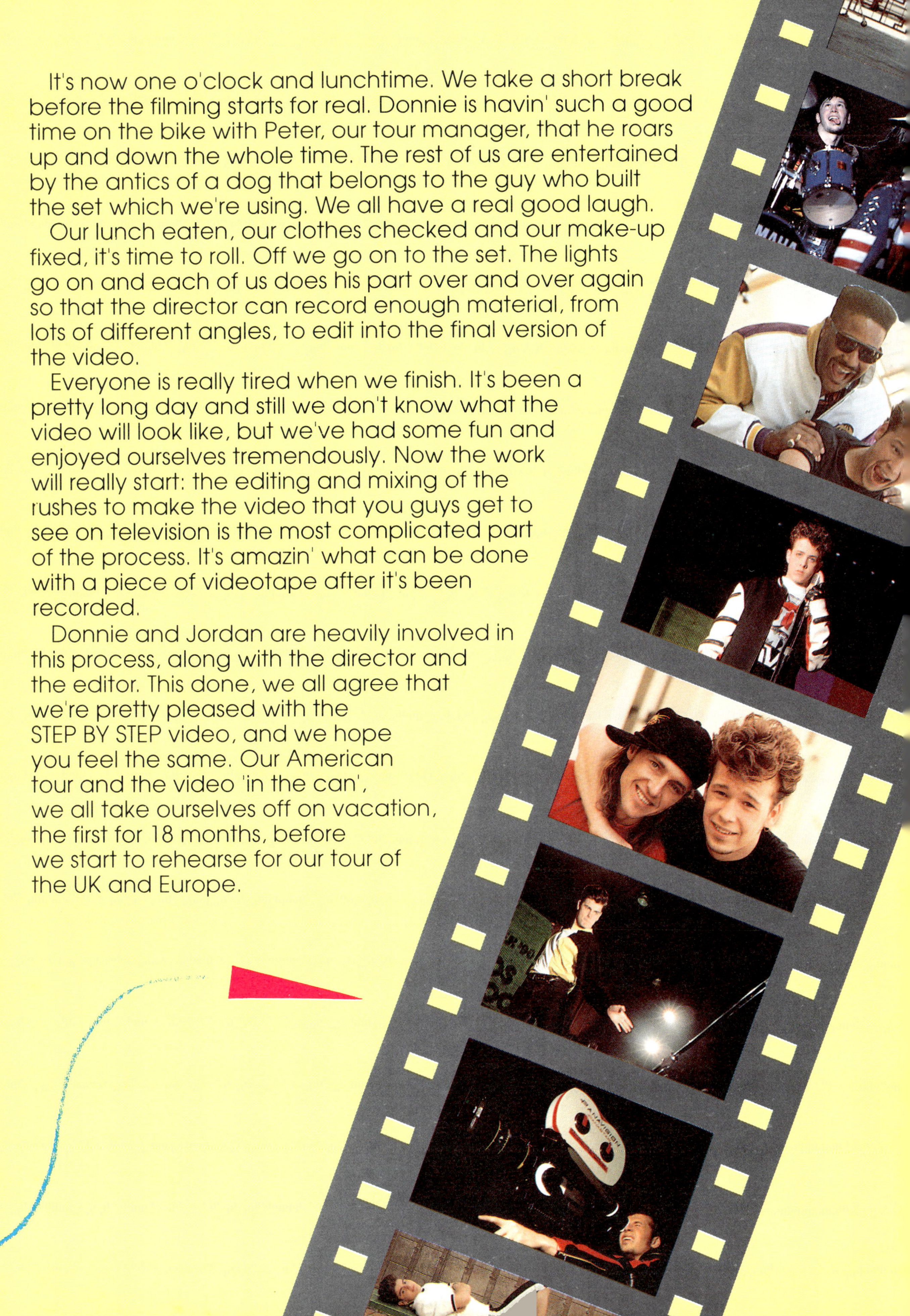

It's now one o'clock and lunchtime. We take a short break before the filming starts for real. Donnie is havin' such a good time on the bike with Peter, our tour manager, that he roars up and down the whole time. The rest of us are entertained by the antics of a dog that belongs to the guy who built the set which we're using. We all have a real good laugh.

Our lunch eaten, our clothes checked and our make-up fixed, it's time to roll. Off we go on to the set. The lights go on and each of us does his part over and over again so that the director can record enough material, from lots of different angles, to edit into the final version of the video.

Everyone is really tired when we finish. It's been a pretty long day and still we don't know what the video will look like, but we've had some fun and enjoyed ourselves tremendously. Now the work will really start: the editing and mixing of the rushes to make the video that you guys get to see on television is the most complicated part of the process. It's amazin' what can be done with a piece of videotape after it's been recorded.

Donnie and Jordan are heavily involved in this process, along with the director and the editor. This done, we all agree that we're pretty pleased with the STEP BY STEP video, and we hope you feel the same. Our American tour and the video 'in the can', we all take ourselves off on vacation, the first for 18 months, before we start to rehearse for our tour of the UK and Europe.

Oriol

WHAT'S DANNY LIKE?

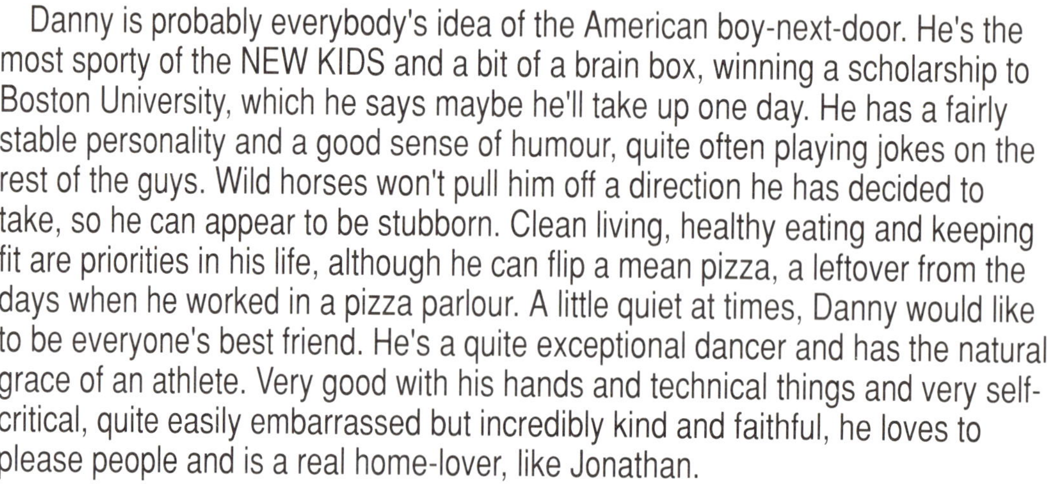

Danny is probably everybody's idea of the American boy-next-door. He's the most sporty of the NEW KIDS and a bit of a brain box, winning a scholarship to Boston University, which he says maybe he'll take up one day. He has a fairly stable personality and a good sense of humour, quite often playing jokes on the rest of the guys. Wild horses won't pull him off a direction he has decided to take, so he can appear to be stubborn. Clean living, healthy eating and keeping fit are priorities in his life, although he can flip a mean pizza, a leftover from the days when he worked in a pizza parlour. A little quiet at times, Danny would like to be everyone's best friend. He's a quite exceptional dancer and has the natural grace of an athlete. Very good with his hands and technical things and very self-critical, quite easily embarrassed but incredibly kind and faithful, he loves to please people and is a real home-lover, like Jonathan.

That's Danny. 

WHAT'S JORDAN LIKE?

A lot of girls think that Jordan is the best looking one in the band, though the others might have something to say about that! Like Donnie, he is a natural leader but in a much quieter fashion. He is the strong silent type, quite tough and brave, and definitely more rebellious than his brother Jonathan. He caused his mother to worry constantly because he used to belong to a pretty wild gang. A serious-minded thinker and a little shy on first meeting people, but he is adaptable and will make the best of most situations, normally seeing the funny side of things. He is into fast living and is a lover of good company, but capable of suddenly changing his mind for no apparent reason. Whilst Jordan could never be called a mother's boy, she is a very important part of his life and quite often when he comes off stage he will phone her just to say 'hi'. Lasagne and ketchup followed by chocolate milkshake is a passion with him so his ideal girl would need to be cute, independent and able to cook a mean pasta. He has a reputation for being a smooth-tongued so-and-so but he really is very modest.

A real heartbreaker, so watch out! 

WHAT'S JONATHAN LIKE?

As the most responsible NEW KID, Jonathan is the one who holds it all together: kind, caring and very reliable, but sometimes a little bossy. Donnie has been known to describe him as a 'Take Charge' kind of guy. Basically a home-loving person, his family mean a lot to him. He's a bit of a romantic; once he finds the right lady he'll stick to her like superglue. He is probably the most fashion-conscious NEW KID and loves shopping for clothes, especially leather jackets. He is an incredibly hard worker, ambitious and decisive, but he has a definitely mystical and dreamy side to his character. Not a loner, he likes the security of other people around him. He's also a lover of animals and has a rare shar pei puppy which he takes almost everywhere with him in the States. Wrinkles (the dog's name) sleeps with Jonathan in his hotel room on a special bunk. Jonathan sometimes gets a bit frustrated with the lack of privacy. "People tend to talk to you about their problems." he says. He is very down to earth. He will admit to complaining a little too much sometimes and can be a little impatient, but he is one of the world's nice guys.

That's what Jonathan is like. 

WHAT'S DONNIE LIKE?

Donnie is the hyper one in the band. He's the guy who whips the audience into a frenzy with all his madcap antics on stage. A natural leader, he is brimming with ideas but will question every rule before he'll obey it. His family are more important to him than himself and he is incredibly loyal. Passionate and a lover of pleasure – but he'd be a very hard man to pin down into a steady relationship. Donnie reckons that he could meet and go out with a girl now who wouldn't have looked at him four years ago. Now she would readily marry him, but that wouldn't suit him at all, though someone who wanted him for himself might stand a chance. NORTH SIDE POSSE are managed by Donnie, who also helps them write their material and acts as sound mixer and recording engineer for them. He's a self-confessed junk food addict, liking nothing more than gorging on Chinese takeaways and Coca Cola, and he loves to play practical jokes on other members of the band and crew. On first meeting, Donnie can appear to be completely mad. He is extremely funny but is known to be moody, and can be a bit of a toughie.

So that's Donnie for you. 

WHAT'S JOSEPH LIKE?

Joseph is a happy-go-lucky sort of guy. He's a bit of a joker and he could charm the birds out of the trees. Sometimes he's a little unsure of himself, but basically he is pretty confident. As a competitive person, winning is very important to him but essentially he is sweet-natured and wouldn't hurt a fly. Show business was probably always going to attract Joseph because from a very early age he loved performing in front of people; he's a little bit of a show-off, in fact. One of his favourite pastimes is shopping and he also loves cars, computer games and videos. He is the youngest member of the band and the only one with blue eyes and though you wouldn't think it to look at him, he is quite a ladies' man already. School work still has to be done, so a tutor accompanies Joseph on the tour bus. If he could have one wish it would be to end all homelessness. If he achieves his ambition to be a politician maybe he'll be able to do something about that.

So that is little Joseph.

A NEW KIDS ON THE BLOCK PLATINUM DISC!!!!

Yo! It may sound too good to be true, but true it is! The NEW KIDS wanna share their success with you so they've decided to give away one of their cool-tough and highly precious platinum discs.

It's for real, and all you have to do to win the disc is answer these five questions:

1 Who manages the band?
2 What is the breed and name of Jonathan's dog?
3 Which NEW KID used to work in a bank?
4 Whose father is Vice-President of the US Bricklayers' Union?
5 Danny had to leave the UK tour after two shows. Why?

Please return your answers before 1st February 1991 to:

The Press Office
c/o Graeme Hill
NKOTB Annual Competition
CBS Records
17-19 Soho Square
London W1V 6HE

Write your answers on a postcard, stating your full name and address. The first correct entry out of the bag will win the NKOTB platinum disc.

NEW KIDS

UK & EUROPE

Monday 23rd April 1990, 10pm

Concorde touched down at London's Heathrow airport. Into the terminal building went our 36-man crew, our management, the band, and us. "We Want New Kids, We Want New Kids," was pretty near the first thing we heard in the UK. Wow, what a welcome! You British Blockheads were sure out in force to let us know that we were in for a really great time on our first ever tour in your country.

Our hotel for the night was just a short ride from the airport and everyone was gonna try real hard to get some shuteye 'cause the journey across the Atlantic can be quite tiring and there was an early start next morning. All of us were really excited; we'd been waitin' a long time for this trip.

KIDS IN THE UK

The morning dawned bright and sunny and while we were still asleep the press, radio and television people gathered to greet us. 8.30am, and in we went for a media welcome, a barrage of questions, flashlights poppin' all over, and all to say that the NEW KIDS ON THE BLOCK had arrived and the 22-day schedule of gigs, television, radio and press interviews was about to get under way.

Edinburgh

The guys in the road crew had gone on ahead to set up the equipment and lights for our first show which would take place in Edinburgh. We were following on by plane after the breakfast media conference. Our arrival in Scotland was another wonderful experience. You guys were going all out to make us feel right at home. Most of us were still pretty bushed, but Joseph wanted to go exploring. He'd never been to visit a real castle, so off he went with a couple of minders, a guidebook in his hand, to take in the sights of Edinburgh Castle whilst the rest of us crashed out again.

On the eve of the gig we were all a little more tense and nervous than usual. Having worked so hard to put the show together, we would now find out what you guys in the UK really thought of us. As soon as we hit the stage we knew that all the effort was gonna be worth it. Fantastic, that's the only way to describe the way you made us feel, and we didn't want to come off stage, but we had to move on. The buses were outside waiting to whisk us off to our next show in Manchester.

Manchester

Everywhere we go folk are always throwin' soft toys and flowers on stage for us; this, however, was Danny's downfall. Just as we started getting into the second song of the night and Danny was doin' some stunnin' dance steps, he slipped on a teddy bear. Danny ain't no wimp and he tried real hard to stay with it, but his ankle was hurt bad and he had to be helped off stage. Dick, our manager, went with him and was told by the doctor that the ankle was very severely twisted.

Meanwhile, that evening's show came to its climax. We trouped backstage to be told that Danny would play no further part in the tour until he'd gotten better, and that the only way that would happen was by restin' his ankle completely for at least three weeks. So it was decided that Danny would return to America. Everyone was pretty upset by this but, hey, this is rock 'n' roll and the show must go on. Off Danny went to catch a plane back to the USA, while the rest of our entourage boarded the buses for the trip to Whitley Bay.

Whitley Bay

Two shows here at the ice rink, and a fabulous reception at both gigs which was great 'cause us four guys were really goin' for it to try to make up for the loss of poor ol' Danny.

Brighton

From Whitley Bay all the way down to Brighton, one real long trek. The weather was wonderful and our hotel rooms there overlooked the sea-front. We could see loads of people sunbathing on the beach. Donnie was standin' on the balcony of his room having a great old chat with a bunch of you guys gathered below. You were screamin' and singin' and chantin' and Jordan was in heaven. We all love to hear you guys havin' a good time but it's a real motivator for him. It was great.

....KIDS IN THE UK....

London

Next day it was back to London to appear on the WOGAN television show. Rehearsals were in the afternoon and when we'd finished we all tucked into burger and chips. All this dashin' about makes you real hungry. Wardrobe and make-up followed with press interviews at the same time. We'd been asked to do a trailer for the evening's show and Terry Wogan joined in pretendin' to be the fifth NEW KID in place of Danny. He's a real funny guy and we had a ball. Can you imagine how thrilled we were when Terry presented us with a double platinum album on the show for sales of HANGIN' TOUGH? We weren't expectin' that. 'Gobsmacked', 'over the moon', 'absolutely knocked out', you say it, we were it. What a great surprise!

It was a little more than hectic getting away after the show and we'd gotten hungry again. So on the way back to the hotel we picked up some good ol' British fish 'n' chips. Hoards of you guys were waiting for us when we arrived and we talked to quite a few folks. We were beginning to recognise faces that kept turning up all over. Jonathan played a bit of a trick on you here, 'cause while you were all at the front of the hotel he quietly slipped out at the back and went for a walk. London has become one of Jonathan's favourite places and he had a great time just wanderin' about.

Paris

The WOGAN show was our last commitment in the UK. We boarded a small private plane and were flown to Paris to do some press and promotion whilst the crew went to Hamburg, Germany to prepare for the first European gig.

Paris is a very beautiful city and we spent most of our first day seeing as much as possible 'cause we knew that the following day was goin' to be pretty frantic again. One of the television shows we did in France was filmed in a park in Paris. That was fun and it made a change from being stuck in a hot and sweaty studio.

KIDS IN EUROPE

Hamburg

3rd, 4th, 5th and 6th May were all concert days in Germany so off we went to Hamburg. After the show, CBS threw a party for us and we were presented with gold discs. A good time was had by all in Germany but we didn't get to visit anywhere 'cause when we weren't travellin' we were sleepin' and when we weren't sleepin' we were doin' a show. All of us are hopin' to go back soon and spend a bit more time there.

Birmingham

Back to the UK and on up to Birmingham for two shows at the NEC. Again, a brilliant reception to each show. You guys were goin' wild and what was real cool was you'd brought along banners sayin' how much you were missin' Danny.

London again

After the final song at the NEC we headed back down country to London. While we were travellin', Peter, our tour manager, came up with the idea of havin' a banner competition in which you had to design and make a banner to wish Danny 'get well soon' and to tell him how much he was bein' missed.

The competition was held outside our record company offices in Soho Square on 10th May and you turned up in droves. It was chaos, but great fun and the banners were fantastic. What a talented bunch you all turned out to be. The winner was goin' to get to speak to Danny by telephone and the runners-up got tickets for the shows in London and a specially made 'Danny's Banner Competition' T-shirt.

That evening we did a guest appearance at Radio 1 on the MARK GOODIER show. You guys were there en masse again and the police had to close the street outside. We slipped in and out of the radio station by a secret door 'cause everyone was a bit worried that someone might get hurt in the crush.

Docklands Arena, London, England was the scene of our final three shows on this trip, the first on Friday, 11th May. This became a non-concert day as there was a massive power cut which couldn't be fixed in time for the show. It could have been real tricky with thousands of you guys stumblin' around in the near darkness. But everythin' turned out ok 'cause nobody panicked, you were all great. It was announced that all ticket holders for that ill-fated show should turn up at the Arena on Sunday lunchtime to see the show that we had called off on Friday. Like everywhere else, the London gigs went down an absolute storm and you guys had made it so wonderful for all of us that it was real hard when it was time to say goodbye.

America Here We Come

Havin' spent so long over here and generally bein' made a fuss of by our friends, it was not without a tinge of sadness that we returned to America. We'd had a real ball and it was just great to see so many of you guys had come to the hotel to see us off. You gave us a right royal send off and all there is left to be said about our first tour of the UK and Europe is thank you for making us so welcome and givin' us such a wonderful time. We had a truly fantastic trip and we'll be back real soon to do some more shows for you. Don't forget, we love ya, each and every one of ya.

YO! BE SEEIN' YA, TAKE CARE.
LOVE FROM
THE NEW KIDS ON THE BLOCK

DONNIE

LEO:
24th July
to 23rd August

The future is still ahead and the present is time for fun. This philosophy could have been written especially for Donnie. The lion is the so-called 'king of the jungle' and as such enjoys the finer things in life and will always have a very comfortable home in which to luxuriate. Even the less well-off Leo will really appreciate a small luxury and absolutely love to be pampered. Donnie is very positive and enthusiastic, a natural-born leader, generous to a fault and very romantic, all of which are strong Leo traits. The big cat can be pompous and intolerant but like the great beast playing with a young cub, full of warmth and loyalty. He will not be happy if his days are dull and boring. A busy and demanding professional life is essential to the lion and will keep him purring with pleasure. His leisure time is also very important to him; just watch your household cat lazily stretching itself under the sun's rays and you will understand why.

JOSEPH

CAPRICORN:
23rd December
to 19th January

Joseph is a fairly typical Capricorn: reliable, determined, stable, and even at his young age he shows great wisdom, although sometimes he can be a little over-exacting. He can be quite serious, a worrier and on occasion a little pessimistic and self-contained. Believe it or not he is prone to bouts of shyness, but has a great sense of humour and an oh so engaging smile, which brings his character into balance. Capricorns usually have fantastic smiles and Joseph is certainly at the top of the pile as far as this is concerned. A rational mind and a ruthless ambition will see that he is successful in his chosen profession. Music and reading are a passion, and patience, which Joseph has plenty of, is a virtue.

JONATHAN

SAGITTARIUS:
23rd November
to 22nd December

Honest, daring, good judgement and great sincerity would describe Jonathan to a T. His love of animals and his straight-talking frankness are other obvious traits. A little careless sometimes, and quite restless, he will always need to feel that freedom is within his grasp as the slightest hint of claustrophobia will drive him to distraction. His enthusiasm for life can occasionally boil over into boisterous behaviour. Being fun-loving and generally optimistic, he might be the sort of guy given to driving fast cars. Jonathan is a very well adjusted kind of guy and has an uncanny ability to store knowledge, which he will put to good use at a later date. He would have made an excellent vet or a writer had superstardom not been his destiny, also perhaps a teacher, since imparting information is well starred for Sagittarians.

TAURUS: 21st April to 21st June

JORDAN

Jordan and Danny were born under the sign of Taurus the bull, so strength and reliability are at the forefront of their characters. Prone to being dogmatic and possessive but extremely affectionate, each will expect a great deal of love from the girls who become their partners. Taureans are lovers of all good things and certainly know how to enjoy them. A great strength of purpose and conviction, coupled with the legendary stubborn streak which all bulls have, will ensure that once these guys have made up their minds to do something, nothing, but nothing, will stand in their way. They have good business sense and very constructive minds. They are artistic yet practical and very good at dealing with matters financial, but are capable of being quite insecure. Taureans hate change of any kind and love to feel totally at home in their surroundings. Bricks and mortar are their security and they adore their houses which will be full of beautiful things. Normally very patient, both Jordan and Danny have high levels of tolerance and are very amiable at most times. But beware, cross the bull and you'll wish that you hadn't!

DANNY

DISCS

UK SINGLES DISCOGRAPHY

Date	Title	Chart position
1989 30th Jan	You Got It (The Right Stuff)	*
8th May	You Got It (The Right Stuff)	74
29th Aug	Hangin' Tough	64
23rd Oct	You Got It (The Right Stuff)	1
27th Dec	Hangin' Tough	1
1990 5th Mar	I'll Be Lovin' You Forever	5
30th Apr	Cover Girl	4
4th Jun	Step By Step	2

UK ALBUMS DISCOGRAPHY

Date	Title	Chart position
1989 27th Nov	Hangin' Tough	2
1990 18th Jun	Step By Step	1

* Didn't chart

US SINGLES DISCOGRAPHY

Year	Title	Chart position
1986	Be My Girl	*
	Stop It Girl	*
	Didn't I Blow Your Mind	8
1988	You Got It (The Right Stuff)	3
	Please Don't Go Girl	10
	Cover Girl	2
	I'll Be Lovin' You Forever	1
	Hangin' Tough	1
1989	Merry Merry Christmas	*
	Funky Funky Christmas	*
	This One's For The Children	7

* Didn't chart

US ALBUMS DISCOGRAPHY

Year	Title	Chart position
1986	New Kids On The Block	25
1988	Hangin' Tough	1
1989	Merry Merry Christmas	9
1990	Step By Step	1

DRAWING

Hows about winning yourself a real chillin' collection of NKOTB goodies! All you have to do is draw or paint a picture of the NEW KIDS, write your full name, age and address on the back and send it to:

Closing date for entries is 1 February 1991

NEW KIDS DRAWING COMPETITION
EDITORIAL DEPARTMENT
WORLD INTERNATIONAL PUBLISHING LTD
PO BOX 111 GREAT DUCIE STREET
MANCHESTER M60 3BL

5 to 10 age group

1ST PRIZE

You win all of these guttin' goodies:
the Hangin' Tough video,
a fabulous NKOTB baseball cap,
a 24-page colour poster programme,
a set of button badges,
AND two incredibly chillin' T-shirts!

COMPETITION

11 to 16 age group
1ST PRIZE

You win an equally chillin' bag of NKOTB merchandise consisting: the Hangin' Tough video, a unique NKOTB watch, a 24-page colour poster programme, a large poster AND two incredibly chillin' T-shirts!

25 RUNNERS UP
in each age group will receive a superb NEW KIDS board game supplied by MB Games.

RULES OF ENTRY

1 Entrants must be between the ages of 5 and 16 years old. Entries are limited to one per person.
2 You must draw the group, not individual members.
3 State your full name, age and address on the back of your entry.
4 All entries will be judged on age and ability. Artistic merit consistent with age of entry will be taken into consideration. The judges' decision is final.
5 Employees and their relatives of World International Publishing and their respective associated companies are not eligible to enter.
6 No cash alternatives or substitute prizes are available.
7 Winners will be notified by post no later than 1 March 1991. A list of winners' names will be available on request providing you send a stamped addressed envelope.
8 We regret that no entries can be returned unless accompanied by a stamped addressed envelope of the correct size.

56 QUESTIONS YOU ALWAYS WANTED TO ASK NKOTB

Q Now you are obviously very famous, how much has it changed your lives?

A Jonathan - Our lives have changed of course, but we are all real close to our families and friends and this helps keep our feet on the ground.

Q Will success go to your heads?

A Donnie - I don't think so. We are just ordinary folk following the direction that our lives are goin' in.

A Joseph - Just hangin' out at home with my friends when I can keeps my head straight.

Q The NEW KIDS ON THE BLOCK have this wholesome image, is it real?

A Donnie - We ain't no saints, the press have given us this wholesome image. We are all very positive people.

Q How do you feel about the girls who throw themselves at your feet?

A Jonathan - Me? I love it!

A Donnie - 20,000 girls screamin' at you is a fantastic feelin'. We enjoy the attention and I could walk out on stage tonight, catch a girl's eyes and fall in love. You never know.

A Danny - Hmm - difficult. If you say in an interview that you like girls with black hair, you upset the girls with blonde hair and so I'm real careful what I say. But basically I have the same ideas and values I've always had.

Q Your first release didn't chart. How did you feel?

A Donnie - We tasted failure. I think it did us good, we know what it feels like.

Q Will your new album be different? If so, how?

A Donnie - Maurice never tries to make us anything that we're not, he takes what we have to offer. He knows exactly what we can all do in the studio. We're growin' up and changin' so our music will develop also. You'll have to wait and see!

A Jordan - We had a great time makin' it! You tell us!

Q NEW KIDS ON THE BLOCK have played their concerts in front of thousands and thousands of people. What is the appeal?

A Jonathan - It's like when kids come to our concerts there are no drinks or drugs - everyone comes just to have a real good time.

A Danny - We and our crew work real hard to make sure people enjoy themselves.

Q Would you consider yourselves the best of friends?

A Joseph - More like brothers. We all still have our own best friends from our schooldays who we like to see when we are at home.

A Danny - Yo!

Q Is it true that Maurice Starr was the band's creator?

A Donnie - Hey man - every band has a creator, someone who has the ideas in the first place. We weren't all thinkin' we could be popstars. Maurice showed us that we could do it and taught us to have confidence in our talent.

A Danny - Maurice lets us sing and dance the way we do it best.

Q How different are the five of you?

A Donnie - Very different. In interviews I say that this is only my opinion and you'll have to ask Jonathan, Jordan, Danny and Joseph for theirs.

A Joseph - We all have different personalities - this is part of the appeal of the NEW KIDS.

Q If you could change places with anyone, who would it be?

A Jonathan - The President of the United States of America. I'd really like to try and clean up the world and make it a better place to live. Everyone has to work together on the problems of pollution - it's a global thing.

Q You guys spend so much time together, do you ever argue?

A Joseph - We are all different people and have our own views on things, so sometimes, yes. But we've been on the road together for so long and we've learned so much about each other that it never becomes a problem.

Q Your fans always try to get to meet you. What is one of the wackiest things they have done to achieve this?

A Danny - We've had them get on to the floor where we're stayin' dressed up as hotel maids. It's weird, sometimes we don't even know where we're staying and still they turn up.

Q When you are on the road, how do you relax?

A Danny - I work out, man.

A Donnie - Ride motorbikes after rehearsals.

A Joseph - Hang out. There are about 60 people on the road with us so not only can you hang out with a different NEW KID every day, but also a different member of the crew.

Q What is your best chat-up line?

A Jonathan - The straightforward approach.- Yo! Get over here!! Ha! Ha!

A Danny - If I really like a girl, I get a bit tongue-tied.

Q If you were shipwrecked on a desert island what would you like to have with you?

A Jonathan - a tough one this - but well - ok, probably lots of things but to start with soap, and food.

Q How do your families feel about your success?

A Danny - Our mothers run the American fan club for us so they're sort of involved, but obviously they're pleased that we're being successful.

A Jordan - We're doin' what we want to do, that makes them happy.

Q You're all still young. Do any of you plan to go back to college?

A Joseph - Yeah. I think I'd like to continue my education although I have a great time while I am on the road.

A Danny - Maybe - I won a scholarship, so maybe.

Q We hear a lot about Biscuit. What does he do for you?

A Jordan - We can't always go out on our own so he looks after us if we want to go shopping or something.

A Joseph - He makes sure we have everything we need.

Q Do you think that the NEW KIDS ON THE BLOCK could have a wider appeal?

A Danny - We do have older fans. I think our music has a pretty wide appeal, especially our Christmas album, the older generation love that one.

A Donnie - Some of our fans are real young so their folks bring them to our concerts and they always seem to have a good time.

PHOTO ALBUM

If you guys want to be the first to know all the news about what's happenin' to us, why don't you write to us at:

NKOTB International Fan Club
PO Box 1270
London
SW4 6QZ

This is the address of our International Fan Club and we would be only too happy to reply and explain how you can receive information on record releases, videos and tours. You'll also get regular newsletters from us on what we've been doin'.

You could be the lucky one who wins one of our competitions - with very special prizes.

Yo! We wanna hear from ya!

NEW KIDS ON THE BLOCK

P.O. Box 1270, London S

BLOCKHEADS ANSWERS

SQUARE

QUIZ

1. North Side Posse
2. Joseph
3. Two
4. Jamie Kelly
5. New Edition
6. Lasagne with ketchup and chocolate milkshake
7. Jonathan
8. Danny
9. Joseph
10. Jonathan
11. Donnie
12. Jordan
13. Danny
14. NEW KIDS' Day

We all hope you've enjoyed reading this annual and we're looking forward to seein' you again real soon!
Thanks for all your love and loyalty.

Donnie W
Yo! Stay cool

You all take care now
Jonathon Knight

Love and Peace

Jordan Knight
Be seein' you real soon

Danny Wood
You guys Hang Tough!

NEW KIDS ON THE BLOCK
NEW KIDS ON THE BLOCK
NEW KIDS ON THE BLOCK
NEW KIDS ON THE BLOCK
NEW KIDS ON THE BLOCK